D0374700

Printed Under License ©2017 Emotional Rescue
www.emotional-rescue.com

Published by Studio Press
An imprint of Kings Road Publishing. Part of Bonnier Publishing
The Plaza, 535 King's Road, London, SW10 0SZ

www.bonnierpublishing.co.uk

Printed in Italy   10 9 8 7 6 5 4 3 2

The Wit & Wisdom of

BEER

"Right, I've got my foreplay sorted out!" he said, "What are you having?"

Having just read so much about the terrible effects of drinking beer, he immediately decided to give up reading.

A s far as he was concerned beer was healthy:
1. Beer comes from hops and barley
2. Hops and barley are plants
3. That makes beer a salad!

He spent around £200 a month on entertainment. Or, as it's more commonly known, beer!

"I really love you!" he said.
"Is that the beer talking?" she asked.
"No, that's me talking to the beer!"

The choice was tricky –
Women or Beer? He'd certainly miss
those special moments, the passionate
times, the love and togetherness that only
the most perfect partner can bring...
"Hmmmm!" he thought,
"How can any woman compete with *that*?!"

He realised he was drinking too much beer when his urine sample had a head on it!

He proved that he did more than just eat, fart and watch the telly. Sometimes he drank beer!

"Just because I smell of beer, I'm six hours late and I parked the car in a hedge you frink I've been drunking don't you?!"

He liked his beer, cars and women exactly the same... With their top off!

He didn't care if the glass was half empty... or half full... as long as there was beer in it!

Even though it was his birthday, he decided to limit himself to just four cans of beer for the day!

He kept saying NO to beer!
However it refused to listen.

There was nothing in life that excited him more than a beer in the fridge he had forgotten about!

He loved his present.
It was always beer o'clock.

He had his 63 inch plasma screen TV and his deluxe shed from B&Q. Now all he needed was a 'beer' fridge!

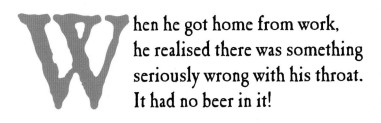

When he got home from work, he realised there was something seriously wrong with his throat. It had no beer in it!

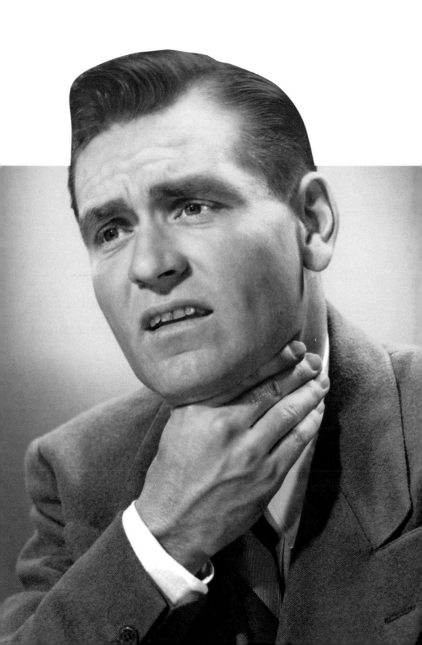

"Get me a beer!" he demanded.
"Have your numbers come up on the lottery?" she asked.
"No," he exclaimed.
"Well get your own beer then!"

Heart pounding, blood flowing and lips pouting... Yep, he had spotted some beers in the fridge.

It wasn't until he met a woman that he realised that these so called 'beer pounds' could be spent anywhere!

You never had to call him. Simply open a beer can and he came running!

This was the last time she would let him organise a romantic dinner.

He only drank beer two times a year...
When it was his birthday and
when it wasn't his birthday!

You could tell he was up for a seriously big night out when he attached his 'Acme Anti-Beer-Spill Cone'.